MONARCH BUTTERFLIES

GROWING READER

LEVEL **3**

700-1500 WORDS

D0047502

KATE WATERS

SCHOLASTIC INC.

New York Toronto London Auckland Sydney
Mexico City New Delhi Hong Kong Buenos Aires

Monarch butterflies are easy to spot. They are large butterflies. They have black heads and bodies with white spots. Their wings are orange with thick black veins. The edges are black and have bright white dots on them.

Dear Family and Friends of New Readers,

Welcome to Scholastic Reader. We have taken more than eighty years of experience with teachers, parents, and children and put it into a program that is designed to match your child's interest and skills. Each Scholastic Reader is designed to support your child's efforts to learn how to read at every age and every stage.

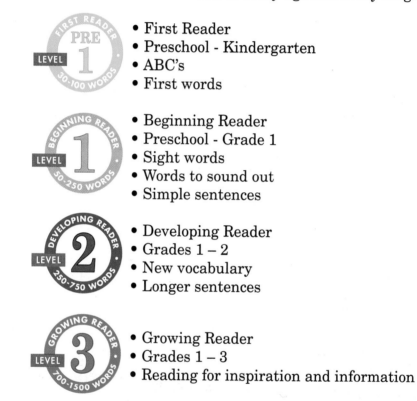

- First Reader
- Preschool - Kindergarten
- ABC's
- First words

- Beginning Reader
- Preschool - Grade 1
- Sight words
- Words to sound out
- Simple sentences

- Developing Reader
- Grades 1 – 2
- New vocabulary
- Longer sentences

- Growing Reader
- Grades 1 – 3
- Reading for inspiration and information

On the back of every book, we have indicated the grade level, guided reading level, Lexile® level, and word count. You can use this information to find a book that is a good fit for your child.

For ideas about sharing books with your new reader, please visit www.scholastic.com. Enjoy helping your child learn to read and love to read!

Happy Reading!

—Francie Alexander
Chief Academic Officer
Scholastic Inc.

ISBN-13: 978-0-545-07234-2
ISBN-10: 0-545-07234-4

Copyright © 2009 by Kate Waters
Book design: Kay Petronio

Expert reader: Donald E. Moore, Associate Director,
Animal Care, Smithsonian Institution's National Zoo

12 11 10 9 8 7 6 5 4 3 2   9 10 11 12 13 14/0

Printed in the U.S.A.
First printing, April 2009

Monarchs are very common in the United States. They live in most parts of the country.

Monarchs go through a series of changes to grow to be adult butterflies. This process is called metamorphosis.

Butterfly eggs
are light green.

A monarch butterfly starts life as a tiny egg. A female butterfly lays the egg on the underside of a milkweed leaf. The eggs are usually safe there because they are so small. Milkweed leaves are a caterpillar's food.

A milkweed plant in flower

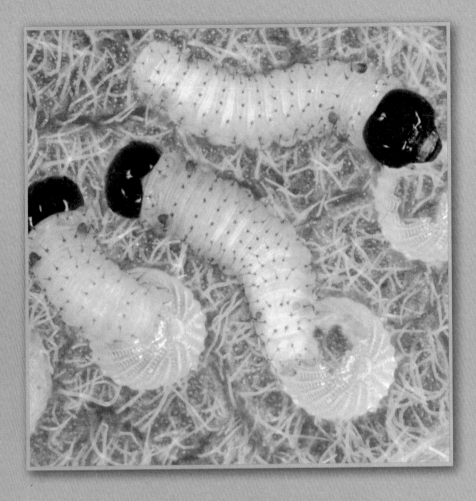

A very tiny caterpillar hatches from the egg after a few days. At first it is so small it can barely be seen. The caterpillar, called a larva, eats the milkweed leaf it was born on first. Then it moves on to eat other leaves.

Soon the caterpillar grows too big for its skin. The old skin splits and falls off. This is called molting. It happens four or five times in two weeks. The new layer of skin underneath is baggy. The caterpillar is ready for its next change when it gets to be two inches long.

The caterpillar squirms out of its old skin.

The caterpillar hangs upside down from a twig or leaf. It curls up so that it looks like the letter "J." A shell grows around the caterpillar. It is light green and has yellow dots on it. This hard shell is called a chrysalis, or a pupa.

The chrysalis becomes almost
clear over the next fifteen days. An
amazing change is happening inside.
A butterfly is forming.

The chrysalis splits apart slowly. The butterfly slips out and hangs on to the shell. Then it opens its wings. Its wings dry and get stiff in a few hours.

Different kinds of butterflies are different sizes and colors. But they all go through metamorphosis. And they all have the same body parts.

The Parts of a Butterfly

Monarch butterflies have long antennae, or feelers. They are used to smell and touch.

A butterfly has compound eyes. That means it can see objects above, below, underneath, and beside it.

Butterflies have six legs. They have taste sensors on their feet.

A curly tube, called a proboscis, leads to the butterfly's mouth. It is used to suck nectar from flowers.

A butterfly thorax is the part that makes its wings and legs move.

Butterfly wings are covered in tiny scales.

Closeup of butterfly scales

The abdomen holds the heart, breathing pores, and most of the digestive system.

15

All butterflies eat nectar. Nectar is a sweet liquid found in flowers. Monarch butterflies are attracted to flowers that are purple or yellow. They only eat during the day.

Butterflies drink
fresh water from
puddles or streams.

Some monarch butterflies hatch in the spring or early summer. They live for only four to five weeks. Other butterflies hatch at the end of the summer. They can live as long as nine months.

These late summer butterflies are called migrant butterflies. To migrate means to travel. These monarchs begin a long journey when the days start to get cool.

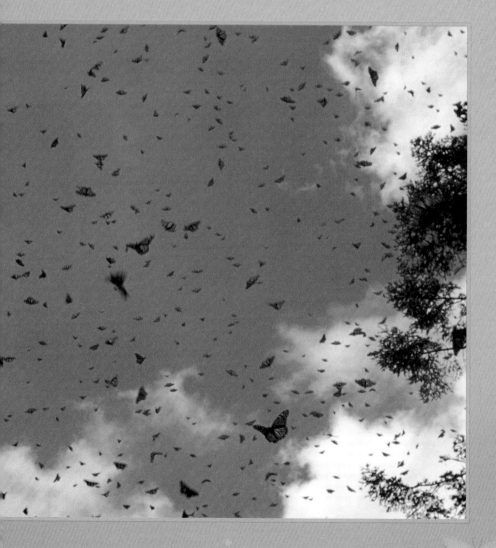

Butterflies cannot move when they get cold. Millions of monarch butterflies fly south in autumn to find warmer weather.

Monarch butterflies are very good gliders. Their wings are four inches wide. Large wings help the butterflies float on currents of air. They stop to rest and eat. They do not fly at night. Yet they can travel up to one hundred miles a day.

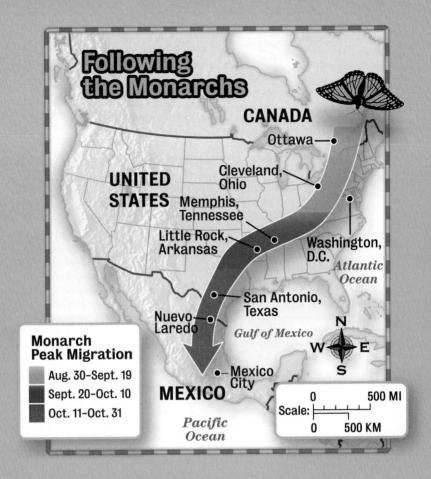

Following the Monarchs

CANADA

Ottawa

Cleveland, Ohio

UNITED STATES

Memphis, Tennessee

Little Rock, Arkansas

Washington, D.C.

Atlantic Ocean

San Antonio, Texas

Nuevo Laredo

Gulf of Mexico

N
W E
S

Mexico City

MEXICO

Pacific Ocean

Monarch Peak Migration

- Aug. 30–Sept. 19
- Sept. 20–Oct. 10
- Oct. 11–Oct. 31

Scale:
0   500 MI
0   500 KM

Most monarchs fly to Mexico. Some fly to southern California or Florida.

The butterflies gather on trees in these warm spots. There can be millions of butterflies on one tree! This is called roosting. They open their wings to catch sunlight and get warm. It can look like the trees are quivering.

Monarch butterflies migrate to the same place their ancestors did. How do they know where to go? That is a mystery that scientists are working to solve.

Scientists track monarch butterfly migration. They capture monarchs and put very small tags on their wings. Then they release the butterflies. People keep track of the tag numbers on butterflies they see. That way scientists can make a map of where a butterfly has been.

Monarch butterflies begin their journey home when spring comes. They fly north to milkweed fields to lay eggs. They have completed their amazing journey.

27

We still have many questions about monarch butterflies. Scientists continue to study them. They help make sure that the places where monarch butterflies roost are being protected. People also make sure that milkweed fields are not cut down or poisoned with weed killer sprays.

Flowering milkweed plants in a field

Some day we may know how monarchs migrate across so many miles to the same places every year. For now, we can enjoy watching these beautiful butterflies all around us.

Glossary

compound—having two or more parts

digestive system—the parts of the body that break down food and get rid of waste

glide—to move by floating on the air

hatch—when a baby animal breaks out of its egg

metamorphosis—the series of changes certain animals go through as they develop from eggs to adults

molt—when an old layer of skin splits and falls off so new skin can grow

nectar—a sweet liquid found in flowers that butterflies eat and bees turn into honey

quiver—to tremble or vibrate

sensor—an area that detects flavor, heat, or sound. Many insects have taste sensors on their feet.